Cooking in the Nude

QUICKIES

Designed by Carolyn Weary Brandt
Edited by Cameron Brown

First published in 1987 by Wellton Books.
Revised, expanded edition copyright © 1995 by Debbie and Stephen Cornwell.

Library of Congress Catalog Card Number 95-80600
ISBN 0-943231-96-5

Printed in Canada
Published by Howell Press, Inc., 1147 River Road, Suite 2,
Charlottesville, Virginia 22901.
Telephone (804) 977-4006
Fourth Printing 1998

HOWELL PRESS

TABLE OF CONTENTS

INTRODUCTION

*Q*UICKIES is for busy but romantic people who love to act out their culinary fantasies. Whenever you need a unique and impressive dinner on short notice, you'll find that a "quickie" is the simple, sensual solution.

Creating a gourmet-quality dinner in less than an hour would challenge even the great chefs. Often, just searching for the right recipe can take that long, but we've saved you the effort. Every recipe in this book can be prepared in an hour or less. How you spend the time you've saved is up to you!

Warning: While impromptu passion in the dining room can be fun, we must advise you to be "Ready for Action" before you start "Fooling Around." Be sure you read both of these sections before you try anything!

QUICKIES is meant to be spontaneous and fun. Just add enough romance and lust to suit your tastes, and enjoy your Epicurean conquest!

READY FOR ACTION
(Presentation)

The most pleasurable quickies are often prompted by chance and impulse! As you're leaving work, you run into an old friend (or make a new one) and extend a dinner invitation for that same evening. Or, you are suddenly overcome with the impulse to practice a little culinary seduction on your spouse. Whatever your motives, there's very little time for planning or preparation. After all, your desire is to lavish attention on your companion, not the kitchen!

But, even when time is tight, the presentation of your Epicurean endeavor is still important. Although your entrée will be enticing on its own, you still need a seductive table setting, the perfect wine, and the right music to bring out the bon vivant in your guest! Be ready for action! You don't have time to waste looking for the candle holders! To be prepared for sudden seductions, we suggest you develop a personalized "Quickie Kit," and store it in a special drawer or corner of a cupboard.

Although you will undoubtedly add your own special touches, your basic "Quickie Kit" should contain the following: two place settings of dinnerware, napkins (prefolded, in rings), placemats or a tablecloth, an ice bucket, wine glasses (red and white), candles and candlesticks, silk flowers and vase, a mini-selection (six bottles) of wine (keep special white wines stored in your refrigerator), and finally, three or four sensuous cassette tapes or CDs. Depending on your style and intentions, you may wish to embellish your kit with a provocative selection of after-dinner pleasures—anything from backgammon to bubble bath. If you're ready for action, you can indulge with confidence!

FOOLING AROUND
(Creating the Mood)

*I*t's 7:00 p.m. and your guest has arrived. Since you're ready for action, you have time for a little fooling around! Naturally, your approach to creating the mood will be tailored to fit the relationship, as well as your fantasies. Whether your dining companion is an old friend, a new acquaintance, or your spouse, we're going to presume that your objectives are romantic. How you're dressed may signal your intentions, so be sure that what you're wearing (or not wearing!) truly reflects just how much fooling around you hope to do.

It takes two to fool around, so involve your guest from the beginning of the evening. Your pre-chosen assortments of wines and music are close at hand. Ask your guest to decant a particular wine, play a special CD, or light the candles. This will enable you to check on the progress of your gourmet quickie and any last-minute garnishes without seeming rushed. Now's the time to "tease and please" with an appetizer, pour the first glass of wine and, during the conversation that follows, reveal the recipe title of your entrée. You've definitely created the mood—where you go from here is up to you!

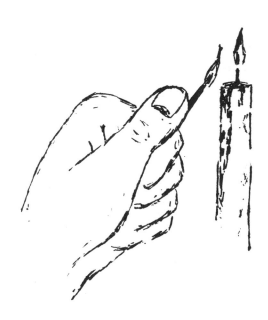

A LICK AND A PROMISE
(The Well-Stocked Pantry)

A candlelight dinner for two,
Will satisfy both of you.
But if you're in a hurry
And we've called for curry,
Replacing with dill won't do!

A well-stocked pantry is a prerequisite to seductive dining on short notice. The following list of seasonings, condiments, and liqueurs will allow you to experiment fully with all of our recipes.

Almonds, slivered	Curaçao	Parsley
Anchovies	Curry powder	Pecans
Anchovy paste	Dill	Pepper, black
Apple cider	Fennel	Pepper, cayenne
Apricots, dried	Garlic, fresh	Pepper flakes
Artichoke crowns, also known as "bottoms" (canned)	Garlic, powdered	Pine nuts
	Ginger, fresh	Poppy seeds
	Ginger, powdered	Port
Artichoke hearts (canned)	Grand Marnier	Raisins
	Hearts of palm	Rosemary
Basil	Kirsch	Sauternes (or dry white wine)
Bay leaves	Knorr Leek Soup (dry)	
Black olives		Sherry
Bouquet Garni (sold as a mixed spice)	Lemons	Soy sauce
	Madeira	Summer savory
Brandy	Marjoram	Tarragon
Brown sugar	Marmalade, orange	Thyme
Butter	Marsala	Vinegar, apple cider
Capers	Mustard, Dijon	Vinegar, balsamic
Caraway seeds	Mustard, dry	Vinegar, red wine
Cashews	Oil, olive	Walnuts
Celery salt	Oil, peanut	Water chestnuts, canned
Chervil	Olives, black	
Chives, fresh	Oregano	Worcestershire sauce
Clam juice	Paprika	

Bits of Pleasure
(Stuffed Shrimp)

20 minutes

8-12 large shrimp,
  shelled and deveined
  (leave tails on)
2 Tbsp. Roquefort or bleu cheese,
  softened
2 Tbsp. cream cheese, softened
1 Tbsp. mayonnaise
1/2 tsp. thyme
1/2 tsp. paprika
1/2 tsp. lemon juice
3 Tbsp. parsley, minced

Drop prepared shrimp in a pot of boiling water and simmer for 3-4 minutes, or until shrimp are pink. Do not overcook. Drain. Cut shrimp lengthwise (do not cut all the way through), leaving tails intact. Blend softened cheeses with all the remaining ingredients, except parsley. Stuff shrimp with cheese mixture. Roll rounded backs of shrimp in parsley. Chill until ready to serve.

Hot Baked Brie

10 minutes

1 Tbsp. butter
1/4 cup almonds or pecans, finely
  chopped
small round Brie cheese

Preheat oven to 350°F. Melt butter over medium heat. Add nuts and sauté for 5 minutes. Using a sharp knife, carefully remove top rind from Brie. Press nuts into soft part of Brie using back of spoon. Bake in covered ceramic or glass dish for 5-7 minutes at 350°F. Serve immediately with crackers or French bread.

Herbed Cheese Fantasy Spread

15 minutes

1/2 lb. Feta cheese
1/2 cup butter, room temperature
1/4 cup green onion, chopped
1/2 tsp. anchovy paste
3/4 tsp. caraway seeds
1/4 tsp. dry mustard

Combine all ingredients, mix thoroughly. Remove mixture to crock, cover, refrigerate. Remove from refrigerator 20 minutes before serving. Serve with assorted crackers.

Crowns of Crab

15 minutes

(Crab-Stuffed Artichoke Bottoms)

1/2 cup fresh crab meat
2-3 Tbsp. mayonnaise
1/4 tsp. Worcestershire sauce
1 Tbsp. lemon juice
cayenne pepper
1 pkg. frozen artichoke bottoms,
   cooked and drained

Mix all ingredients, except artichokes, together thoroughly. Stuff prepared bottoms with mounds of crab mixture, cover and chill until ready to serve.

French Dip

(Leek Dip in a French Bread Bowl)

Step One:

1/2 pkg. Knorr Leek Soup

1 bunch green onions,
   tops only, chopped

1 cup mayonnaise

1 cup sour cream

1 can water chestnuts, drained
   and chopped

1 pkg. frozen chopped spinach,
   cooked and squeezed dry

garlic powder to taste

Combine all ingredients together thoroughly.

Step Two:

round loaf French bread

Cut a "lid" from top of loaf. Scoop out bread from inside leaving 1" thickness on sides and bottom. Fill with dip. Replace lid, place on serving tray.

Step Three:

4-5 large carrots, peeled and cut
   into sticks

1/2 head broccoli, cut into florets

1/2 head cauliflower, cut into florets

2 zucchini, cut into sticks

Surround bread with vegetables and serve.

Lover's Leaves

10 minutes

(Baby Lettuces)

This is a light salad composed of assorted baby lettuces, sold as "spring mix" or "mesclun" in better produce departments.

1/3 lb. "spring mix"

Gently wash baby lettuces and pat dry. Arrange in serving bowl or on individual plates, and dress with Balsamic Splash (p. 19) or Voulez-Vous Vinaigrette (p. 19).

Spontaneous Salad

10 minutes

(Mixed Greens)

Heartier than the delicate Lover's Leaves, this mixed green salad goes well with any of the dressings in this book.

1/4 head romaine
1/2 head endive
1/2 bunch arugula

Wash lettuce and break into bite-size pieces. Arrange in serving bowl, and dress just before serving.

Caesar and Please Her

(Caesar Salad)

The timing is perfect now to "Caesar and Please Her." The deliciously romantic ritual of a true Caesar salad could be the culinary coup that seals her fate. We'll show you how!

Step One:

4 slices homemade-style white bread,
   crusts removed
butter
1/4 tsp. garlic powder

Preheat oven to 400°F. Butter both sides of bread. Sprinkle with garlic powder. Trim to 1/2" cubes. Spread on baking sheet, bake at 400°F until golden, 10-15 minutes.

Step Two:

1 egg

Bring 2" water to boil in small pan. Turn heat off. Add egg to pan, let stand 30 seconds. Remove with spoon to bowl of cold water.

Step Three:

1 clove garlic, cut in half
1/3 cup olive oil
2-3 anchovies, chopped
1 tsp. Worcestershire sauce
1/2 tsp. salt
freshly ground pepper to taste
1/4 tsp. dry mustard
1 large bunch romaine lettuce,
   torn into bite-size pieces
1 lemon, cut in half
1/3 cup Parmesan cheese, grated

Rub inside of wooden bowl with garlic. Add oil, anchovies, Worcestershire sauce, salt, pepper, and mustard. Stir. Add romaine, toss until leaves are glistening. Break egg into salad, squeeze lemon halves through cloth napkin into salad and toss thoroughly again. Add croutons and cheese, toss lightly, and serve.

To assure the ultimate suave and debonair presentation, we suggest you pre-measure all ingredients while she is sipping her wine and reflecting on your sensitive and gentle nature. Little does she know that you are about to "Caesar and Please Her!"

Suggestive Salad

(Spinach, Pear, and Pine Nut Salad with Raspberry Vinaigrette)

Step One:

1/2 bunch spinach leaves, washed
   and torn into bite-size pieces
1 pear, skinned and cut into
   bite-size chunks
1/4 cup pine nuts, toasted

Arrange ingredients on chilled salad plates.

Step Two:

1/2 cup raspberries
1/2 cup light olive oil
1/4 cup apple cider vinegar
1 egg yolk
1/4 tsp. Dijon mustard
1/8 tsp. ground ginger

Purée raspberries in blender or food processor. Add remaining ingredients, blend well. Chill until ready to use.

Creamy Honey-Lemon Dressing

5 minutes

This dressing lends itself to endless variations.

2/3 cup mayonnaise

2 Tbsp. vegetable oil

2 Tbsp. honey

2 Tbsp. half-and-half

1 Tbsp. prepared mustard

1 1/2 Tbsp. fresh lemon juice

1/8 tsp. dry mustard

1 Tbsp. parsley, chopped

Combine all ingredients and mix thoroughly.

For extra panache, you may want to add some of the following to a salad served with Creamy Honey-Lemon Dressing:

1/8 tsp. curry

1 green onion, chopped

1/2 tsp. celery seeds

1/2 tsp. poppy seeds

1-2 tsp. sesame seeds

2 Tbsp. raisins

2 Tbsp. nuts, slivered almonds, chopped pecans, cashews, or walnuts

2 tsp. capers

2 tsp. chopped black olives

Balsamic Splash

5 minutes

(Balsamic Vinaigrette)

1 Tbsp. balsamic vinegar
1 tsp. sugar
1 tsp. Dijon mustard
2 1/2 Tbsp. extra virgin olive oil
salt and pepper

Whisk sugar in balsamic vinegar until dissolved. Add mustard, stir to blend, then add olive oil and whisk until thick. Add salt and pepper to taste.

Voulez-Vouz Vinaigrette

5 minutes

(Classic Vinaigrette)

1 Tbsp. red wine vinegar
1 tsp. Dijon mustard
3 Tbsp. light olive oil
1/2 tsp. tarragon, chives, or oregano
   (optional)
salt and pepper

Whisk vinegar and mustard together. Add herbs, if desired. Whisk in olive oil. Add salt and pepper to taste.

Halibut My Place?

30 minutes

(Halibut in Caper Cream Sauce)

. . . or your place is fine, wherever you dine you'll have plenty of time!

Step One:

2 8-oz., 1"-thick halibut steaks
1 Tbsp. butter
salt and pepper

Preheat oven to 450°F. Arrange halibut in individual au gratin dishes or baking dish. Melt butter and brush over halibut, season to taste. Bake at 450°F for 20 minutes.

Step Two:

1/4 cup slivered almonds
1 Tbsp. butter

Melt butter, add almonds and sauté until golden, approximately 10-15 minutes. Keep warm.

Step Three:

2 Tbsp. butter
2 Tbsp. flour
1/2 cup milk
2 Tbsp. sherry
1/2 cup sour cream
2 Tbsp. fresh lemon juice
2 Tbsp. capers, drained
parsley
lemon slices

Melt butter over medium heat, whisk in flour, and cook for 2 minutes. Whisk in milk, stirring constantly until thickened. Remove from heat. Blend in sherry, sour cream, lemon juice, and capers. Pour over fish. Garnish with sautéed almonds, parsley, and lemon slices.

Teasing and Pleasing

French Dip

Love 'em and Leaf 'em

Spontaneous Salad with

Voulez-Vous Vinaigrette

Fast au Fares

Halibut My Place?

Making Time

Garlic-Rosemary Potatoes

Wine

Pinot Blanc

♥ *Lover's Lure*

(Trout Fillets in Grand Marnier Sauce)

Once the lure is set, control your lines, and play with your catch as long as you like!

Step One:

2 trout, boned and halved

1/2 cup butter

1/4 cup flour

1-2 Tbsp. fresh lemon juice

1/2 lemon, sliced

Melt butter over medium-high heat in large frying pan. Put flour in plastic bag, add trout, one at a time. Shake to coat. Place in pan skin side up, brown 5 minutes. Sprinkle lemon juice over trout. Add lemon slices to pan. Turn trout and brown 1-2 minutes. Remove trout and lemons to heated platter.

Step Two:

3/4 cup Grand Marnier

1/3 cup butter, cut into pieces

2 Tbsp. parsley, chopped

Pour off any butter in pan, add Grand Marnier. Shake pan so that it is evenly coated with the liqueur, turn heat to low. Using a long match, ignite Grand Marnier. Allow flames to subside. Whisk butter pieces into pan until sauce thickens. Pour a little sauce over trout, sprinkle with parsley. Pour remaining sauce into serving bowl and pass separately.

Teasing and Pleasing

Bits of Pleasure

Love 'em and Leaf 'em

Spontaneous Salad with Creamy Honey-Lemon Dressing

Fast au Fares

♥*Lover's Lure*

Making Time

Bacon Cauliflower Sauté

Wine

Chenin Blanc

A Grape Fantasy

(Salmon and Scallops with Grapes and Cashews)

... may turn your fantasies into reality!

Step One:

2 Tbsp. butter

2 salmon fillets, skinned

Melt butter in frying pan, over medium-high heat. Sauté salmon fillets 2-3 minutes per side until they barely flake when tested. Transfer salmon to warm platter, cover loosely, keep warm.

Step Two:

2 Tbsp. butter

1/2 cup seedless Thompson grapes

1/3 cup cashews

8 large ocean scallops

1/4 cup dry white wine

1 Tbsp. lemon juice

1/2 tsp. tarragon

Add butter to pan, sauté grapes, cashews, and scallops until scallops are no longer translucent. Add wine, lemon juice, and tarragon; heat through. Spoon mixture over salmon fillets and serve immediately.

SUGGESTED MENU

Teasing and Pleasing

Hot Baked Brie

Love 'em and Leaf 'em

Suggestive Salad

Fast au Fares

A Grape Fantasy

Making Time

Lemon Rice

Wine

Alsatian Pinot Gris

or Pinot Noir

♥Cop A Fillet

35 minutes

(Snapper Fillets in Ginger Cream Sauce)

. . . and this won't be your only success tonight!

Step One:

1/2 cup Sauternes or dry white wine
1/2 medium onion, thinly sliced
1 bay leaf
1/8 tsp. thyme
1/2 cup whipping cream

Combine all ingredients, except cream, in saucepan and boil until reduced to about 2 Tablespoons. Reduce heat and add cream. Simmer until mixture coats spoon, approximately 2-3 minutes. Remove bay leaf.

Step Two:

1/2 cup butter, cut into pieces
1/2 clove garlic, crushed
1/4 tsp. fresh ginger, minced
1/8-1/4 Tbsp. parsley, minced
1/2 tsp. soy sauce
salt and pepper

Stir butter, one piece at a time, into cream mixture until blended. Add remaining ingredients. Keep warm.

Step Three:

2 Tbsp. butter
2 snapper fillets
salt and pepper

Melt butter in large frying pan. Season fillets with salt and pepper to taste and fry them on both sides over medium heat, until lightly browned and opaque throughout. Fish should flake easily when done.

Step Four:

curly leaf lettuce leaves
2 Tbsp. chopped parsley
3 Tbsp. slivered almonds
lemon wedges

Arrange lettuce leaves on plate. Top with fillets. Spoon sauce over fish. Sprinkle with parsley and almonds. Garnish with lemon.

SUGGESTED MENU

Teasing and Pleasing

Crowns of Crab

Love 'em and Leaf 'em

Lover's Leaves with Balsamic Splash

Fast au Fares

♥Cop A Fillet

Making Time

Asparagus in Almond-Lemon Butter

Wine

Fumé Blanc

♥Give A Little, Get A Little

35 minutes

(Shrimp in Wine Sauce au Gratin)

Be a little shellfish and get all that you can!

Step One:

1/4 cup butter

1 clove garlic, minced

1 Tbsp. parsley, minced

1 tsp. Bouquet Garni

2 tsp. lemon peel, grated

1/2 cup dry bread crumbs

1/4 cup Parmesan cheese

salt and pepper

Preheat oven to 325°F. Melt butter in large frying pan. Sauté garlic for 2 minutes. Remove pan from heat and add remaining ingredients, toss to coat bread crumbs well. Salt and pepper to taste. Set aside.

Step Two:

2 Tbsp. butter

2 Tbsp. flour

1 cup half-and-half or milk

2 Tbsp. sherry

salt and pepper

Melt butter over medium heat. Whisk in flour and cook 2 minutes. Whisk in half-and-half, stirring constantly until thickened. Whisk in sherry. Salt and pepper to taste.

Step Three:

1 lb. large shrimp, shelled and deveined

Drop prepared shrimp into boiling water and simmer 3-4 minutes, or until pink. Do not overcook. Arrange shrimp in au gratin dishes or a baking dish. Top with sauce, then bread crumbs. Bake at 325°F for 20 minutes.

Teasing and Pleasing

French Dip

Love 'em and Leaf 'em

Caesar and Please Her

Fast au Fares

Give A Little, Get A Little

Making Time

Bacon Cauliflower Sauté

Wine

Chenin Blanc

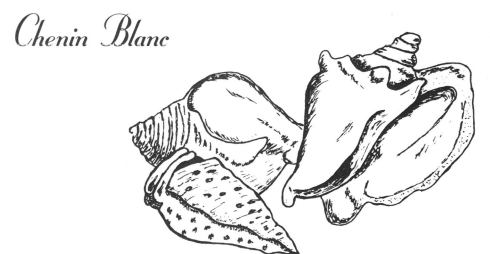

Promiscuous Prawns

(Scampi in Garlic-Wine Sauce)

*A dinner of scampi and a good bottle of wine have been known to loosen one's inhibitions—
just how loose is up to you!*

Step One:

2-3 Tbsp. olive oil

1 clove garlic, minced

2-3 green onions, chopped

8-10 large prawns, cleaned and
   butterflied

2/3 cup Sauternes or dry white wine

juice of 1/2 lemon

2 Tbsp. parsley, chopped

2-3 Tbsp. butter

Heat oil in large frying pan over medium
heat. Sauté garlic and onions until tender.
Add prawns and sauté until pink, approximately 3 minutes. Add remaining ingredients, butter last. Stir until creamy.

Step Two:

lemon wedges

parsley sprigs

Warm au gratin or serving dish, arrange
scampi, and garnish with lemon and
parsley.

Teasing and Pleasing

Crowns of Crab

Love 'em and Leaf 'em

Spontaneous Salad with

Honey-Lemon Dressing

Fast au Fares

Promiscuous Prawns

Making Time

Brussels Sprouts in Garlic-Parmesan Butter

Wine

Sauvignon Blanc

Casual Encounters

(Crab and Artichokes in Madeira Cream Sauce)

. . . are the best kind, and with the right partner, this one could be fantastic!

Step One:

1 1/2 cups shell macaroni

Preheat oven to 350°F. Cook pasta until barely al dente and drain.

Step Two:

1/4 cup butter

3 green onions, chopped

2 Tbsp. flour

1 1/2 cups half-and-half

1/4 cup Madeira

salt and pepper

Melt butter in large frying pan over medium heat, add onions and sauté 3-4 minutes. Whisk in flour and cook 2-3 minutes. Turn heat to low, whisk in half-and-half, turn heat to medium, continue stirring until sauce thickens. Turn heat to low, whisk in Madeira. Salt and pepper to taste. Keep warm.

Step Three:

1 Tbsp. lemon juice

2 cups fresh crab meat

1 8-oz. can artichoke hearts, drained

3/4 cup Gruyère or Swiss cheese, grated

Toss crab with lemon juice. In au gratin dishes or baking dish, layer well-drained macaroni, artichoke hearts, crab, half the cheese, the sauce from Step Two, and remaining cheese. Bake at 350°F for 25 minutes.

Teasing and Pleasing

Hot Baked Brie

Love 'em and Leaf 'em

Lover's Leaves with

Balsamic Splash

Fast au Fares

♥Casual Encounters

Making Time

Asparagus in

Almond-Lemon Butter

Wine

Pinot Blanc

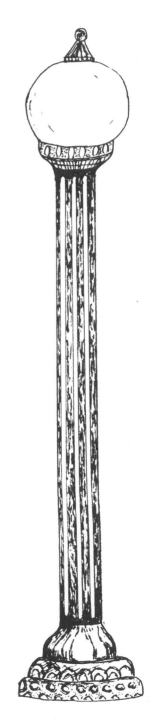

Ménage à Trois

(Sole Stuffed with Scallops, Crab, and Shrimp)

This erotic combo of three seafoods will encourage a lusty appetite!

Step One:

1 Tbsp. butter
4 fillets of sole, patted dry
10 small scallops
3/4 cup crab meat
3/4 cup small cooked shrimp
1/2 cup Monterey Jack cheese, grated

Preheat oven to 450°F. Butter individual au gratin dishes. Place one fillet on bottom of each dish, top with half the scallops, crab, shrimp, cheese, and second fillet. Set aside.

Step Two:

1/2 cup butter
2 egg yolks
1 Tbsp. lemon juice
1/2 tsp. dry mustard
1/8 tsp. salt

Melt butter. Place remaining ingredients in bowl of a mixer. With mixer on high, slowly add butter in a steady stream until sauce is thickened and creamy. Pour sauce over fillets and bake at 450°F for 10-15 minutes.

Step Three:

2 Tbsp. parsley, chopped
paprika

Sprinkle parsley over stuffed fillets and dust with paprika.

Teasing and Pleasing

Bits of Pleasure

Love 'em and Leaf 'em

Spontaneous Salad with Almonds, Snow Peas, and Honey-Lemon Dressing

Fast au Fares

♥ *Ménage à Trois*

Making Time

Broccoli in Orange Butter

Wine

Gewürztraminer

Skinny Dippin' Shrimp

(Rich Shrimp Chowder)

Clothes are optional—or set your own rules—for an evening of pleasure, this is just one of the tools!

Step One:

2 Tbsp. butter

6-8 green onions, chopped

1 clove garlic, minced

Melt butter in large saucepan over medium heat. Add onions and garlic. Sauté until tender.

Step Two:

2 10 1/2-oz. cans cream of potato soup

1 8-oz. pkg. cream cheese, softened

2 cups milk

cayenne pepper

Stir soup and softened cream cheese into onion mixture until smooth. Add milk and season with cayenne pepper to taste, blending well.

Step Three:

2 cups shrimp, cleaned and deveined

1 8-oz. can whole kernel corn, drained

Drop prepared shrimp into boiling water and simmer 3-4 minutes, or until pink. Do not overcook. Add shrimp and corn to soup mixture, bring to a boil. Turn heat to medium-low and simmer 10 minutes. Serve.

Teasing and Pleasing

Hot Baked Brie

Love 'em and Leaf 'em

Caesar and Please Her

Fast au Fares

♥ Skinny Dippin' Shrimp

Bread

Crusty French Bread

Wine

Dry Chenin Blanc

♥ Chicken Porno Bleu

45 minutes

(Roquefort-Stuffed Breasts in Wine and Herb Sauce)

Be careful! This variation of a classic could result in an "R-rated" end to the evening!

Step One:

2 oz. Roquefort or bleu cheese, softened

6 oz. cream cheese, softened

1 clove garlic, minced

3 Tbsp. butter

1 Tbsp. brandy

Preheat oven to 350°F. Blend garlic and cheeses together, do not overmix. Add butter and brandy and blend well.

Step Two:

1 large chicken breast, skinned, boned, and halved

Cover breast halves with wax paper and flatten with mallet until 1/4" thick. Place half the cheese mixture on each breast and carefully fold breasts in half to encase filling. Place stuffed breasts on dinner plate, cover with waxed paper, and place 2-3 salad plates on top to weight. Refrigerate for 20 minutes.

Step Three:

1 egg, beaten

1/3 cup flour

3/4 cup seasoned bread crumbs

Dip breast in flour, then in egg, then roll in crumbs. Place in individual au gratin dishes and bake 20 minutes at 350°F.

Step Four:

3 Tbsp. butter

1/2 tsp. each basil, chervil, fresh chopped parsley

1/3 cup Sauternes or dry white wine

Melt butter, add herbs and wine. Bring mixture to slow boil. Pour over breasts and serve.

Teasing and Pleasing

Bits of Pleasure

Love 'em and Leaf 'em

Suggestive Salad

Fast au Fares

♥*Chicken Porno Bleu*

Making Time

Asparagus in Almond-Lemon Butter

Wine

Riesling

Fowl Play

30 minutes

(Chicken Breasts with Artichoke Cream Sauce)

Holding is definitely not a foul in this game. In fact, the only possible penalty is for holding back!

Step One:

1 3/4 cup chicken stock
1/2 cup onion, chopped
3/4 cup heavy cream

Put stock and onion in heavy saucepan over high heat. Boil until reduced to 3/4 cup. Whisk in cream, and boil until reduced to 1 cup.

Step Two:

10 large artichoke bottoms
2 tsp. fresh lime juice
salt and pepper

Purée artichoke bottoms in blender. Add cream sauce, lime juice, salt, and pepper. Blend briefly. Pour back into pan, keep warm.

Step Three:

2 large chicken breasts
olive oil
salt and pepper
lime wedges

Rub chicken breasts with oil. Season with salt and pepper to taste. Grill or barbecue 5 to 6 minutes per side, or until springy to the touch. Serve on warm plates with artichoke sauce and garnish with lime.

Teasing and Pleasing

Herbed Cheese Fantasy Spread

Love 'em and Leaf 'em

Lover's Leaves with Balsamic Splash

Fast au Fares

Fowl Play

Making Time

Asparagus in Almond-Lemon Butter

Wine

Semillon or Gewürztraminer

Veni, Vidi, Vici

(Chicken Breasts with Artichoke Hearts and Mushrooms)

I came, I saw, I conquered; you, too, will say the same!

Step One:

3 Tbsp. flour

2 chicken breasts, boned, skinned,
   cut into 1/2"-wide strips

3 Tbsp. vegetable oil

Put flour in plastic bag, add chicken strips, and shake to coat. Heat oil in frying pan over medium heat. Add chicken and sauté until golden. Remove to warm plate, keep warm.

Step Two:

1/4 cup butter

1 tsp. garlic, minced

4-6 oz. artichoke hearts, sliced

8-10 medium mushrooms, sliced

1/2 cup dry white wine

1 Tbsp. lemon juice

salt and pepper

1 tsp. parsley, minced

Pour off oil in pan. Add butter, melt over medium heat. Add garlic, artichoke hearts, and mushrooms. Sauté for 5 minutes. Add wine, lemon juice, and salt and pepper to taste; mix thoroughly, and simmer for 5 minutes. Place chicken in warmed au gratin dishes or serving platter. Spoon sauce over chicken and serve immediately.

SUGGESTED MENU

Teasing and Pleasing

French Dip

Love 'em and Leaf 'em

Caesar and Please Her

Fast au Fares

Veni, Vidi, Vici

Making Time

Lemon Rice

Wine

Sauvignon Blanc

♥ Lust at First Bite

(Stuffed Chicken Breasts with Banana Grand Marnier Sauce)

Lust at first bite, as well as first sight, might make this a lingering, sensual night!

Step One:

1 large chicken breast, skinned, boned, and halved

salt and pepper

Preheat oven to 350°F. Cover chicken with wax paper and flatten breasts with mallet. Season inside and out with salt and pepper to taste.

Step Two:

1 medium ripe banana, mashed

1/3 cup Grand Marnier or orange curaçao

1 1/2 tsp. lemon juice

1/4 cup dark corn syrup

1/4 tsp. salt

Mix all ingredients together and set sauce aside.

Step Three:

1/4 cup butter

1/4 cup walnuts, chopped

2 Tbsp. raisins

1/8 tsp. salt

1/8 tsp. pepper

1/2 cup soft bread crumbs

Melt butter. Add remaining ingredients and toss to blend. Place half the stuffing on one end of each breast, roll meat around filling, and secure with a toothpick. Place stuffed breasts in au gratin dishes. Pour half the banana Grand Marnier sauce over chicken and bake at 350°F for 25-30 minutes, basting once.

Step Four:

1/2 banana, sliced

Top breasts with sliced bananas and spoon remaining sauce over chicken. Return to oven for 2-3 minutes and serve.

Teasing and Pleasing

Hot Baked Brie

Love 'em and Leaf 'em

Lover's Leaves with Balsamic Splash

Fast au Fares

♥Lust at First Bite

Making Time

Julienne of Carrots and Apricots

Wine

Gewürztraminer

A Quick Caper

(Chicken Breasts in Caper-Madeira Sauce)

A quick caper like this one will leave you and your guest plenty of time for any other capers you have in mind!

Step One:

2 chicken breasts, skinned and
  boned
1/4 cup flour
1 tsp. salt
1/2 tsp. paprika
1/4 tsp. pepper

Cover breasts with wax paper and flatten with mallet until 1/4"-thick. Combine flour and spices in plastic bag, add breasts, one at a time, and coat well. Shake off excess.

Step Two:

3 Tbsp. butter
1 Tbsp. olive oil

Heat butter and oil in frying pan until bubbling. Add chicken breasts and sauté over medium-high heat, 2-3 minutes per side. Remove to heated platter.

Step Three:

2-4 Tbsp. Madeira
2-3 Tbsp. fresh lemon juice
3 Tbsp. capers, drained
3 Tbsp. parsley, chopped
2 Tbsp. lemon zest

Add Madeira to oil/butter and stir to loosen bits at bottom of pan. Add lemon juice and capers, heat through. Pour over chicken breasts, sprinkle with parsley and lemon zest. Serve immediately.

SUGGESTED MENU

Teasing and Pleasing

Crowns of Crab

Love 'em and Leaf 'em

Spontaneous Salad with Voulez-Vous Vinaigrette

Fast au Fares

A Quick Caper

Making Time

Bacon Cauliflower Sauté

Wine

Chenin Blanc

A Passionate Pair

(Nouvelle Chicken Cordon Bleu with Warm Tomato Relish)

A passionate pair, in any affair, can do what they dare. Dare him!

Step One:

1/4 cup leeks, minced

1 Tbsp. vegetable oil

1/2 cup tomatoes, peeled and
  chopped

1 Tbsp. Madeira

sugar, salt, and pepper

Heat oil in frying pan over medium heat, add leeks and sauté until tender and golden. Add remaining ingredients and season to taste with sugar, salt, and pepper. When mixture begins to simmer, turn heat to low and keep warm.

Step Two:

2 chicken breasts, boned, skinned,
  and pounded to 1/4" thickness

1 Tbsp. vegetable oil

1 Tbsp. butter

2 thin slices prosciutto or other
  smoked ham

Heat butter and oil in frying pan over medium-high heat. Sauté chicken breasts, turning once, for approximately 3 minutes. Remove to warmed au gratin dishes or serving platter. Add ham to pan and cook, turning, until it begins to brown. Place one slice ham over each chicken breast.

Step Three:

2 slices mozzarella cheese

2 Tbsp. parsley, minced

Heat broiler. Place one slice of cheese over each breast. Broil until cheese melts and begins to bubble. Spoon tomato relish over breasts. Sprinkle with parsley and serve immediately.

Teasing and Pleasing

Herbed Cheese Fantasy Spread

Love 'em and Leaf 'em

Suggestive Salad

Fast au Fares

A Passionate Pair

Making Time

Garlic-Rosemary Potatoes

Wine

Spanish Rioja

It Had To Be Ewe

(Medallions of Lamb in Rosemary-Brandy Sauce)

Make it known who you have in mind when you serve this entrée.

Step One:

3-4 meaty 1"-thick lamb loin chops,
    boned to create medallions
1/2 tsp. rosemary
salt and pepper
flour
2 Tbsp. butter
2 Tbsp. olive oil

Season medallions with rosemary and salt and pepper to taste. Dust with flour. Melt butter and oil in frying pan and brown lamb over medium-high heat, until cooked to taste, approximately 15 minutes.

Step Two:

2 Tbsp. flour
1 cup beef stock
1 tsp. rosemary
salt
1/2 cup heavy cream
1 Tbsp. brandy
1 tsp. chopped parsley

Remove medallions to warmed au gratin dishes or plates. Over medium heat, whisk flour into pan juices. Cook for 2 minutes. Whisk in stock. Add rosemary and salt to taste. Over medium-high heat, add cream and stir until thickened. Add brandy and pour sauce over meat. Garnish with parsley.

Teasing and Pleasing

Crowns of Crab

Love 'em and Leaf 'em

Spontaneous Salad with

Creamy Honey-Lemon Dressing

Fast au Fares

♥*It Had To Be Ewe*

Making Time

Brussels Sprouts in

Garlic-Parmesan Butter

Wine

Fumé Blanc

Affaire Thee Well

(Medallions of Lamb in Wine Sauce with Sautéed Vegetables)

. . . but never tell. This quickie could lead to more than a one-night stand.

Step One:

2 zucchini, cut into julienne
  matchsticks
1 small onion, sliced

Cook zucchini and onion in boiling water until crisp-tender. Drain and plunge into ice water. Drain.

Step Two:

3-4 1"-thick lamb loin chops, boned
  to create medallions
salt and pepper
3-4 Tbsp. Dijon mustard
1/3 cup port
1/2 cup vegetable broth

Season lamb with salt and pepper to taste. Brush lightly with mustard. In nonstick frying pan, brown medallions over high heat, turning once, until done. Remove to heated plate and keep warm. Deglaze pan with port and reduce liquid to 2 Tablespoons. Add broth and simmer until reduced by half.

Step Three:

5 Tbsp. olive oil
3 cloves garlic, minced
6 artichoke bottoms, julienned
2 tomatoes, peeled and coarsely
  chopped
5 mushrooms, sliced
1/2 cup black olives, sliced

Over medium-high heat in large frying pan, sauté garlic in olive oil until just wilted. Add remaining vegetables. Add zucchini and onion from Step One. Sauté 5-10 minutes. Arrange on heated plates and top with lamb.

Step Four:

2-3 Tbsp. butter

Whisk butter into sauce from Step Two. Add juices left on plate from lamb. Pour over lamb and vegetables.

Teasing and Pleasing
Hot Baked Brie

Love 'em and Leaf 'em
Suggestive Salad

Fast au Fares
Affaire Thee Well

Making Time
Garlic-Rosemary Potatoes

Wine
Sauvignon Blanc

Tempting Tender Loins

(Pork and Apples Glazed with Kirsch)

The most pleasurable way to overcome a temptation is to yield to it.

Step One:

2-3 pork loin chops 1"-1 1/2" thick,
   boned
salt and pepper

Preheat oven to 350°F. Season meat with salt and pepper to taste. In nonstick frying pan, over high heat, sear tenderloins on both sides. Remove to baking dish.

Step Two:

1 cup brown sugar
2/3 cup Kirsch
1/2 cup apple cider

Combine ingredients in saucepan. Cook over medium-high heat, stirring constantly for 2 minutes. Spoon sauce over meat and bake 25 minutes at 350°F.

Step Three:

2 Tbsp. butter
1/2 cup sliced almonds

Sauté almonds in butter until golden, approximately 10-15 minutes.

Step Four:

1 Tbsp. butter
2 large apples, sliced thickly
1/2 cup Sauternes or dry white wine
1 tsp. powdered ginger

Melt butter over medium heat. Add apples and sauté briefly. Add wine and ginger, continue cooking until apples are tender.

Step Five:

Remove tenderloins to au gratin dishes and top with apple slices. Pour sauce over all and sprinkle with almonds.

SUGGESTED MENU

Teasing and Pleasing

Bits of Pleasure

Love 'em and Leaf 'em

Lover's Leaves with

Balsamic Splash

Fast au Fares

Tempting Tender Loins

Making Time

Julienne of Carrots and Apricots

Wine

Riesling

A Saucy Affair

(Pork Tenderloins in Sour Cream Sauce)

A saucy affair may be yours tonight. But be sure you're ready for more than fooling around!

Step One:

2-3 pork tenderloin chops, boned
salt and pepper
1/2 tsp. marjoram
2 Tbsp. olive oil

Preheat oven to 350°F. Season tenderloins on both sides. Heat oil in frying pan over high heat and brown tenderloins. Remove to au gratin dishes or baking dish.

Step Two:

2 Tbsp. butter
1/2 onion, minced
8-10 mushrooms, sliced
2 Tbsp. flour
1 cup Sauternes or dry white wine
1 beef bouillon cube
1/2 cup sauerkraut, undrained
1 cup sour cream
1/2 tsp. marjoram

To same pan add butter, heat until sizzling. Add onion and mushrooms and sauté until tender. Lower heat to medium and add flour, cook 2 minutes. Add wine and beef boullion cube, stirring until dissolved. Add remaining ingredients, blending well. Pour sauce over tenderloins and bake at 350°F for 45 minutes to 1 hour.

Teasing and Pleasing

Herbed Cheese Fantasy Spread

Love 'em and Leaf 'em

Spontaneous Salad with

Voulez-Vous Vinaigrette

Fast au Fares

A Saucy Affair

Making Time

Garlic-Rosemary Potatoes

Wine

Sauvignon Blanc

Consuming Passions

(Veal Scallopine in Rich Cream Sauce)

This selection has never failed to live up to its name.

Step One:

1/4 cup flour

salt and pepper

2-4 veal loin chops, boned and
    flattened to 1/4" thickness to form
    scallopine

4 Tbsp. butter

Preheat oven to 425°F. Combine flour and salt and pepper to taste in a plastic bag. Add veal scallopine one at a time, and coat well. Shake off excess flour. Heat butter over medium-high heat and brown veal on both sides, approximately 1-2 minutes per side. Remove veal to au gratin dishes or plates and keep warm.

Step Two:

2 leeks, chopped

2 shallots, minced

6-8 mushrooms, chopped

3 oz. (about 1/2 cup) ham, cut into
    strips

2 Tbsp. flour

1 cup milk

salt and pepper

Sauté leeks and shallots until almost tender, add mushrooms and sauté briefly, until tender. Add ham, stir in flour, then slowly add milk, stirring constantly. Bring mixture to a slow boil. Lower heat. Continue stirring until thickened. Add salt and pepper to taste.

Step Three:

3/4 cup Gruyère or Swiss cheese,
    grated

Sprinkle half the cheese over veal, pour half the sauce over it, then layer the remaining cheese and sauce. Bake 15 minutes at 425°F.

SUGGESTED MENU

Teasing and Pleasing

Crowns of Crab

Love 'em and Leaf 'em

Spontaneous Salad with

Voulez-Vous Vinaigrette

Fast au Fares

♥*Consuming Passions*

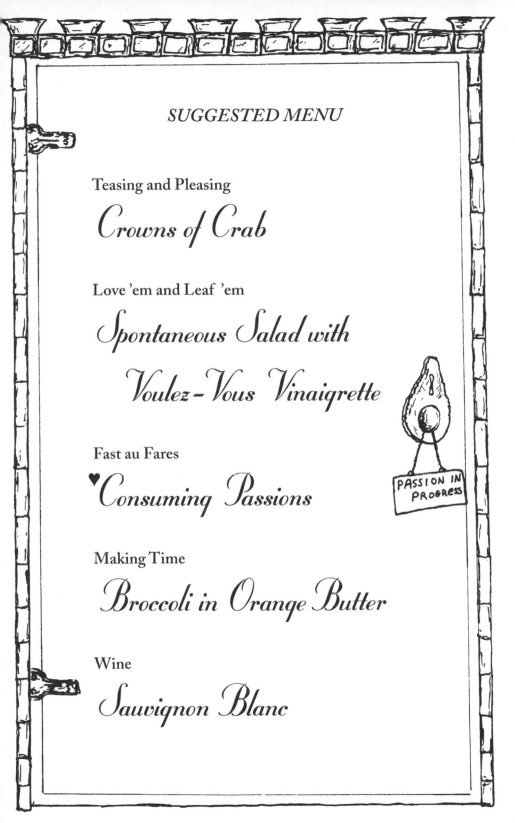

PASSION IN PROGRESS

Making Time

Broccoli in Orange Butter

Wine

Sauvignon Blanc

Vealing Lusty?

(Veal and Ham Rolls in Tomato Basil Sauce)

. . . or vealing loving? Reveal your true vealings tonight!

Step One:

2-3 veal scallops (8-10 oz. total
   weight), pounded to 1/8" thickness

2-3 thin slices proscuitto or other
   smoked ham, cut to fit scallops

1/4 cup flour

2 Tbsp. butter

2 Tbsp. olive oil

Place a slice of proscuitto over each scallop. Roll scallops, securing with toothpicks. Dust with flour. Heat oil and butter in frying pan, add rolls and sauté over medium-high heat until browned. Remove veal rolls to heated platter.

Step Two:

2 leeks, chopped

1 shallot, minced

1/2 cup Sauternes or dry white wine

1/4 cup Marsala or Madeira

2 tomatoes, peeled and chopped

2 tsp. basil

salt and pepper

Add leeks and shallots to skillet, sauté over medium heat until tender, about 5 minutes. Stir in wine and Marsala, bring to a boil, then turn heat to low. Return veal to pan. Stir in tomatoes and basil; add salt and pepper to taste. Cover and simmer 20 minutes. Remove veal to au gratin dishes or plates and spoon sauce over all.

SUGGESTED MENU

Teasing and Pleasing

Herbed Cheese Fantasy Spread

Love 'em and Leaf 'em

Lover's Leaves with Balsamic Splash

Fast au Fares

Vealing Lusty?

Making Time

Bacon Cauliflower Sauté

Wine

Pinot Blanc

Veal You Or Von't You?

(Veal in Mushroom Cream Sauce)

Only your true love knows for sure!

Step One:

1/3 cup plus 2 Tbsp. dry white wine

1/2 tsp. fresh lemon juice

1/8 tsp. salt

8-10 mushrooms, thinly sliced

2 Tbsp. butter

1 tsp. flour

Combine 3 Tablespoons of the wine, the lemon juice, and salt in small frying pan. Add mushrooms. Cover and cook over medium-low heat until mushrooms are tender. Add butter to pan and gradually sprinkle in flour, stirring until thickened. Remove from heat.

Step Two:

2 Tbsp. butter

1 shallot, minced

2 leeks, chopped

2-3 veal loin chops, boned to form scallops and pounded to 1/4" thickness

Melt butter in large frying pan, over medium-high heat. Add shallots and leeks, sauté until tender, about 2-3 minutes. Add veal and quickly brown, about 1-2 minutes. Remove veal to warmed au gratin dishes or plates. Add wine remaining from Step One to pan, scraping up brown bits. Add deglazed pan juices to mushroom sauce.

Step Three

1/2 cup whipping cream

lemon juice

salt and pepper

2-3 Tbsp. parsley, chopped

Place mushroom sauce over medium-high heat, add cream and boil approximately 2 minutes or until thick and reduced by 1/4. Add lemon juice and salt and pepper to taste. Pour sauce over veal, sprinkle with parsley.

Teasing and Pleasing

French Dip

Love 'em and Leaf ' em

Spontaneous Salad with

Voulez-Vous Vinaigrette

Fast au Fares

Veal You Or Von't You?

Making Time

Brussels Sprouts in

Garlic-Parmesan Butter

Wine

Gamay Beaujolais

Fondue Me, Please!

(Beef Fondue with Mushroom-Madeira Sauce)

With a gentle caress, this dish could lead from a "maybe" to a "yes."

Step One:

1 lb. lean tenderloin of beef, trimmed of fat and cut in bite-size cubes

Mound beef cubes on dinner plates, cover and refrigerate.

Step Two:

2 Tbsp. butter
2 green onions, thinly sliced
1 leek, thinly sliced
3 cups mushrooms, finely diced
1/2 cup Madeira
1 10 1/2-oz. can beef broth

Melt butter in large saucepan, add green onion, leek, and mushrooms and sauté until tender. Add Madeira and broth and simmer over medium-high heat approximately 5 minutes, or until reduced by half.

Step Three:

2 Tbsp. butter
2 Tbsp. flour
salt and pepper

Melt butter in small frying pan over medium-low heat. Whisk in flour and cook 2 minutes. Add roux to mushroom mixture, stirring until sauce thickens. Season with salt and pepper to taste. Serve in individual small bowls.

Step Four:

peanut oil
1/4 cup butter

Pour oil into fondue pot until 1/3 full. Add butter. On stove, heat until sizzling. Transfer pot to fondue stand, light flame, keep hot.

Teasing and Pleasing

Hot Baked Brie

Love 'em and Leaf 'em

Lover's Leaves with Balsamic Splash

Fast au Fares

Fondue Me, Please!

Making Time

Garlic-Rosemary Potatoes

Wine

Cabernet Sauvignon

Schuss Kabobs

45 minutes

(Marinated Orange Beef with Pineapple)

Get a fast start on the evening with a downhill race that could let you finish on top!

Step One:

1/4 cup orange marmalade

1/2 cup fresh-squeezed orange juice

2 Tbsp. curaçao

1 tsp. prepared mustard

1/2 tsp. curry powder

1/4 tsp. garlic powder

Combine marinade ingredients in small saucepan over medium heat. Cook until marmalade melts, stirring frequently.

Step Two:

1 lb. lean sirloin

1 orange

1 cup fresh pineapple, cut into bite-size pieces

oil

Preheat grill or broiler. Slice meat across grain into strips 1" wide, 4" long, and 1/4" thick. Cut oranges crosswise into 1/2" thick slices, then cut each slice like a pie into bite-size wedges. Thread a piece of meat onto skewers, accordian-style. Then thread a piece of orange onto the skewer, then a piece of meat, then pineapple. Repeat until all skewers are full. Brush grill with oil. Grill or broil kabobs until done, basting frequently with marinade. Serve immediately.

SUGGESTED MENU

Teasing and Pleasing
Herbed Cheese Fantasy Spread

Love 'em and Leaf 'em
Lover's Leaves with Balsamic Splash

Fast au Fares
♥*Schuss Kabobs*

Making Time
Garlic-Rosemary Potatoes

Wine
Pinot Noir or Zinfandel

Seductive Steak

(Grilled Steak Salad)

. . . a lovely cool salad for those sizzling summer nights!

Step One:

1 lb. London Broil or flank steak, trimmed

Broil or grill steak 3-4 minutes per side; it should be rare. Cool, then slice into thin strips across the grain. Wrap tightly and refrigerate.

Step Two:

1 clove garlic, minced

1 1/2 tsp. Dijon mustard

1/2 tsp. tarragon

2 Tbsp. red wine vinegar

1/2 tsp. sugar

1/2 cup extra virgin olive oil

salt and freshly ground pepper

Mix garlic, mustard, tarragon, and vinegar in a small bowl. Add sugar and stir until dissolved. Slowly whisk in olive oil. Add salt and freshly ground pepper to taste.

Step Three:

1 cup hearts of palm, sliced

1 cup pitted black olives

1/2 Vidalia onion, sliced

1 bunch watercress or arugula, cleaned

1 ripe tomato, cut into wedges

Place steak in a large bowl and toss with dressing. Add hearts of palm, olives, and onions and mix again. Add greens, toss lightly, and serve on a platter garnished with tomatoes.

SUGGESTED MENU

Teasing and Pleasing

Hot Baked Brie

Fast au Fares

♥Seductive Steak

Bread

Crusty French Bread

Wine

Gamay Beaujolais

A Tempting Proposition

(Stir-Fried Beef and Scallops)

Make her an offer she can't refuse!

Step One:

1 cup water
1 Tbsp. fresh ginger, sliced
1 Tbsp. freshly ground pepper
1/2 tsp. red pepper flakes
1-1 1/2 tsp. salt

Combine all ingredients in small saucepan and bring to a boil. Reduce heat and simmer 10 minutes.

Step Two:

2 Tbsp. peanut oil
2 cloves garlic, minced
1 lb. beef tenderloin, trimmed and
  cut into strips 1/2" thick and
  halved crosswise
3/4 lb. fresh ocean scallops
2-4 oz. snow peas
1 cup green onions, sliced diagonally
2 Tbsp. liquid from Step One
1/4 tsp. soy sauce
pinch red pepper flakes

Heat oil in wok or large frying pan, until almost smoking. Add garlic, beef, scallops, and snow peas. Stir-fry approximately 1 minute. Add remaining ingredients and stir-fry 30 seconds longer. Spoon into warmed au gratin dishes (or serving bowl) and serve immediately.

Teasing and Pleasing

Crowns of Crab

Love 'em and Leaf 'em

Spontaneous Salad with Creamy

Honey-Lemon Dressing

Fast au Fares

A Tempting Proposition

Making Time

Broccoli with Orange Butter

Wine

Merlot

 Fetish-ini

(Fettucine Primavera)

Who knows what fetishes lurk in your true love's heart? Do you?

Step One:

8 slices bacon, chopped

Fry bacon until crisp. Remove with slotted spoon and drain on paper towels.

Step Two:

1/2 lb. fettucine
1/4 cup butter

Cook fettucine al dente. Drain and toss with butter in large serving bowl. Set aside, keep warm.

Step Three:

3-5 mushrooms, sliced
1 large carrot, sliced
1/2 cup cauliflower, sliced
1/2 cup frozen peas
1 medium zucchini, sliced
4 green onions, sliced
1 clove garlic, minced

Add vegetables to bacon drippings in frying pan and sauté over medium-high heat until crisp-tender.

Step Four:

4 egg whites
1/4 cup whipping cream
1 cup fresh Parmesan cheese, grated
salt and pepper to taste

Beat egg whites and cream together until blended. Toss with fettucine. Add vegetables, bacon, Parmesan cheese, salt and pepper, toss again.

Teasing and Pleasing

Herbed Cheese Fantasy Spread

Love 'em and Leaf 'em

Caesar and Please Her

Fast au Fares

Fetish-ini

Wine

Pinot Noir

♥ Game, Set, Match

25 minutes

(Linguine with Scallops in Avocado Cream Sauce)

Your ace service in the dining room could earn you the advantage sooner than expected. Go for match point tonight.

Step One:

1 medium avocado
3 Tbsp. dry white wine
2 tsp. lime juice
1/2 tsp. chervil
1/2 tsp. basil
1/2 tsp. tarragon
1/4 tsp. dill
1/8 tsp. garlic powder

Using blender or food processor, purée all ingredients until smooth.

Step Two:

Cook linguine al dente, drain.

Step Three:

1 Tbsp. butter
1/2 lb. scallops
1 clove garlic, minced
1/4 cup heavy cream

Melt butter in large frying pan over medium heat, and sauté garlic and scallops until scallops become opaque. Add avocado mixture and heat through. Stir cream into mixture, taste, and adjust seasonings. Toss with linguine and serve on warm plates. Garnish with lime wedges. Add salt and pepper to taste.

SUGGESTED MENU

Teasing and Pleasing

Bits of Pleasure

Love 'em and Leaf 'em

Lover's Leaves with

Balsamic Splash

Fast au Fares

♥*Game, Set, Match*

Wine

Chablis

♥ Mission Im-pasta-ble

(Spaghetti with Pesto)

Should you decide to accept this mission, the rest of the world will disavow any knowledge of you and your lover's existence for the next 24 hours. Make the most of it!

Step One:

2 cups fresh basil leaves
1/2 cup olive oil
2 Tbsp. pine nuts
2 cloves garlic
1/2 tsp. salt

Combine ingredients in a blender or food processor and purée.

Step Two:

1/2 cup Parmesan cheese, freshly grated
2 Tbsp. Romano cheese, freshly grated
2 Tbsp. butter, softened

Pour purée into a bowl and, using a wooden spoon, mix in the two cheeses. When the cheese is completely incorporated, beat in the softened butter. Set aside.

Step Three:

salt
water
1/2 lb. spaghetti

Bring large pot of salted water to a boil. Add spaghetti and cook al dente. Drain.

Step Four:

1 Tbsp. pine nuts, chopped
2 ripe plum tomatoes, diced
fresh basil leaves

Pour pasta into serving bowl. Spoon pesto over pasta. Garnish with fresh basil leaves, pine nuts, and tomatoes.

Teasing and Pleasing

Crowns of Crab

Love 'em and Leaf 'em

Spontaneous Salad with

Voulez-Vous Vinaigrette

Fast au Fares

♥Mission Im-pasta-ble

Bread

Crusty French Bread

Wine

Pinot Grigio

# Mussel Beach

(Linguine with Mussels and Clams)

Getting buffed for the beach is gratifying when your sweetheart is undenying.

Step One:

1 Tbsp. olive oil

3 cloves garlic, minced

2 8-oz. bottles clam juice

1 cup white wine

3 cups water

1/2 tsp. each basil, oregano,
   marjoram, and thyme

salt

1/2-3/4 lb. linguini

Sauté garlic in olive oil in stockpot over medium heat. Add remaining ingredients, except pasta, and bring to a boil. Add salt to taste. Add pasta, bring back to a boil, stirring to separate, until cooked al dente, about 10-14 minutes. Drain and divide into two large shallow bowls.

Step Two:

1 Tbsp. olive oil

3-4 cloves garlic, minced

Heat oil in small (5 qt.) stockpot over medium heat. Add garlic and sauté. Turn heat off.

Step Three:

12-18 New Zealand cockles (or
   small steamer clams), scrubbed

12-18 mussels, scrubbed and
   debearded

1 8-oz. bottle clam juice

1/2 cup Sauternes or dry white wine

1/4 cup butter

1/2 tsp. each marjoram, summer
   savory, thyme, fennel

1 tsp. each basil, oregano

1 pinch ground red pepper

2 Tbsp. fresh parsley, chopped

Add remaining ingredients to stockpot with garlic, cover, turn heat to medium, steam 5 minutes. Serve over pasta with plenty of French bread to dip in the sauce.

Teasing and Pleasing

Hot Baked Brie

Love 'em and Leaf 'em

Caesar and Please Her

Fast au Fare

♥Mussel Beach

Bread

Crusty French Bread

Wine

Chablis

Bacon Cauliflower Sauté

15 minutes

Step One:

4-5 slices bacon, chopped

In large frying pan over medium-high heat, fry bacon until crisp. Remove with slotted spoon and drain on paper towels.

Step Two:

1/2 head cauliflower, cut into florets
1/2 tsp. celery salt
1 Tbsp. fresh chives, chopped

Sauté cauliflower in bacon drippings over medium heat until lightly browned on all sides. Add celery salt and toss. Remove to serving bowl. Toss with bacon and chives.

Broccoli in Orange Butter

20 minutes

Step One:

1 head broccoli, broken into florets
1/2 cup orange juice

Steam broccoli until just tender. Meanwhile, in small saucepan over medium-high heat, reduce orange juice to 2 Tablespoons.

Step Two:

4 Tbsp. butter
1 Tbsp. orange peel, grated
1 Tbsp. leek, minced

Melt butter in frying pan over medium-low heat. Add leek and orange peel. Sauté until tender. Blend reduced orange juice into orange peel-leek mixture. Add broccoli and toss gently to coat. Serve immediately.

Garlic-Rosemary Potatoes

30 minutes

2 large baking potatoes, peeled and
  sliced 1/2-inch thick
1/4 cup butter
2-3 Tbsp. rosemary, crushed
garlic salt
pepper

Preheat oven to 375°F. Spread potatoes on greased baking sheet. Melt butter and brush half the butter on potatoes. Sprinkle with rosemary and garlic salt and pepper to taste. Bake at 375°F until golden, approximately 10 minutes. Turn, brush with remaining butter, season with rosemary and garlic salt and pepper to taste, and bake until golden and crisp.

Brussels Sprouts in Garlic-Parmesan Butter

Step One:

1/2 lb. Brussels sprouts, washed and
  trimmed

Steam sprouts until tender, about 15
minutes. Keep warm.

Step Two:

2 Tbsp. butter

1 clove garlic, minced

1/4 cup fresh Parmesan cheese,
  grated

salt and pepper

Melt butter in frying pan over medium
heat. Sauté garlic 2 minutes. Drain
sprouts, add to butter, toss to coat evenly.
Add Parmesan, toss again. Season with
salt and pepper to taste, toss again.
Remove to serving bowl.

Lemon Rice

1 cup rice
1 egg
2 Tbsp. lemon juice
2 Tbsp. Parmesan cheese, grated
2 Tbsp. parsley, minced

Prepare rice according to package directions. Just before serving, combine remaining ingredients in bowl and mix well. Stir mixture into hot rice and blend well.

Asparagus in Almond-Lemon Butter

25 minutes

Step One:
1/2 lb. pencil-size asparagus spears

Steam asparagus until crisp-tender. Arrange on serving platter and keep warm.

Step Two:
1/4 cup butter
1/4 cup sliced almonds
1 Tbsp. lemon juice

Melt butter in saucepan over medium heat. Sauté almonds until golden. Add lemon juice and blend well. Spoon over asparagus, and serve immediately.

Julienne of Carrots and Apricots

20 minutes

2 Tbsp. butter

1 shallot, cut into strips

1/2 lb. carrots, cut into julienne
   matchsticks

6 dried apricots, cut into strips

1/2 cup vegetable or chicken broth

1 Tbsp. apple cider vinegar

Melt butter in frying pan over medium-high heat. Add shallot and sauté until tender. Add carrots and apricots and sauté 2-3 minutes. Add stock, cover and simmer until carrots are crisp-tender. Uncover and simmer until all liquid evaporates. Sprinkle with vinegar.

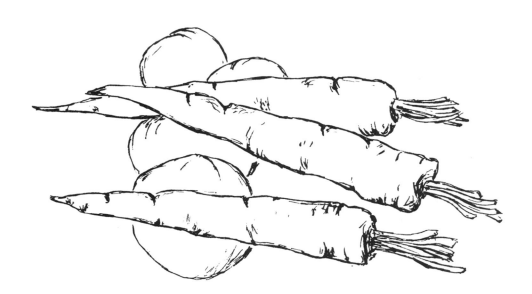

SUBJECT INDEX

Fish

Lamb

Veal

Vegetables

RECIPE INDEX

T

V

FLEETING FANTASIES

(Notes)

FLEETING FANTASIES
(Notes)

FLEETING FANTASIES
(Notes)

FLEETING FANTASIES
(Notes)